I0406642

Copyright 2014 by J.J. Jones - All rights reserved.

In no way is it legal to reproduce, duplicate, or transmit any part of this document in either electronic means or in printed format. Recording of this publication is strictly prohibited and any storage of this document is not allowed unless with written permission from the publisher. All rights reserved.

Table of Contents

Introduction

I want to thank you and congratulate you for purchasing the book, Debt Free Forever The Ultimate Guide to "Knowing Nothing to Having Everything in Financial Freedom, Becoming a Millionaire, and Becoming Debt Free Forever".

This book contains proven steps and strategies to get you out of debt, help you stay out of debt, and then lead you to financial stability.

This three step process is essential. This is because, much like anything else you do in life, you should not stop at the halfway point. And that is what getting out of debt really is! The other part of being debt free is to become financially stable, so much so that you can live a fulfilling life, afford an adequate lifestyle, and be free from the limitations that your current financial status, shackles you in!

To be perfectly up front, there is no secret formula that is too good to be true. All there is to becoming debt free is knowing what has worked for hundreds of debt ridden consumers. Learning to tweak what works to fully fit your situation. Then, following through with your personalized debt free road map. And making sure you do not repeat the mistakes of your debt ridden past!

Thanks again for purchasing this book, I hope you enjoy it!

Chapter 1: Why and How Deep are You in Debt?

Before you can determine what type of plan will work for you, first you need to determine the reasons you got into debt in the first place. Be absolutely honest with yourself here! This is because, the efficacy of the plan you utilize, is determined by the accuracy and truth of your assessment. Tip: take your time when making the assessment. Dig deep, and add notes to your list of debts, i.e. was it a failed endeavor, a home foreclosure, a foolish spur of the moment splurge, or a necessary expense like hospitalization fee, did you lose your job, etc.

Debt Free Journal

At this point, you want to dedicate a notebook, journal, or electronic file for your entire journey. This way you know where you are starting from. You can constantly monitor where you are at. And, you fix your eye on that debt free goal.

Accumulated Debt?

How long did it take you to get to this low point? This realization can help you better assess, the reason for your financial woes. For example: you started incurring debt as soon as you lost your job. You tried to make ends meet with a part time job, and kept up appearances by charging heavily on your credit card.

How Much Exactly?

List down "ALL" your debts. It would help a lot if you could list them down from the most interest accruing, oldest debt, biggest single debt amount, etc. Make sure to have a separate sum for: due and demandable debts; about to be due (1 month or less), future collectibles, etc. Tip: if you know how to use Microsoft Excel, or any similar computer program, this should make your life a lot easier!

30% Rule

If you take 30% of your monthly income (assuming you have income), How long will it take for you to pay for all your debts? This should provide you with a rough estimate. Of course, if you have disposable, liquid assets, then the timeframe should be accelerated.

Chapter 2: Income vs. Expenses

An income vs. expense worksheet is necessary for you to determine how much of your income are you spending. You can utilize your I&E worksheet in several ways. This includes but is not limited to:

- Knowing how much you actually spend vis a vis how much of that spending you can cut off.

- Knowing how much income you still need

- Pinpointing the area where you spend the most and then determining whether or not it coincides with your priorities.

Common sense says that you can spend as much as you make in a month. But common sense is not very practical. That is, if you want to get out of debt and eventually earn millions.

30% Surplus

In reality, it is a good idea to save up at least 20% to 30% of your monthly net income. Leave that untouched and deposit it in your savings account for a rainy day! Anything below 20% and you are overspending way beyond your means, or you are not earning enough income.

Sources of Income

"ALL" sources of income must be considered. From your salary, income on rental property, interest income, etc.

What Income to Include?

If you are the sole provider for the household, then you include your total net income. This is gross income minus taxes. If you have another member of the household who fully shares his/her income to the household i.e. spouse, then add their net income as well.

If another member of the family shares only part of their income, then only add that to the total net income. Make sure to only include regular contributions. For example:

Mr. A 2,000 net monthly

Mrs. A 1,500 net monthly

Son A 300 monthly contribution

Total Expenses

For accurate results it would be best if you had receipts for your expenses. Tip: if you enroll certain accounts online, then you have easy access to your tabulated expenses i.e. Credit cards.

Miscellaneous Expenses

Make sure to include all expenditures. For example: miscellaneous expenses that you might have overlooked. This includes paper money you had to exchange or buy gum or buy bottled water with, for spare coins you need. You then whittle away at your expenses until you only have spare change for unnecessaries and 99% of your spending is fully identifiable.

Tip: any money you can't account for, when balancing your income and expenses goes to miscellaneous. This way you actually see how much of a sinkhole your unnecessary expenses are.

Savings Account

You need to deposit that 30%, preferably more of your income on a bank account. This gets credited to your list of expenses. This way you are creating a good credit standing with your bank, to offset, at least to a certain extent, other declared debts you might have. Perform a general cleaning in your home and collect all your spare and unnecessary change. Deposit these as well!

Tightening the Belt

Look at your income and expense worksheet. Try to remove anything or minimize any and every area in your spending. For example:

Minimize takeout and start cooking meals. Minimize meat purchases and balance it out with fruits and veggies. Stop buying fizzy and sugary drinks. All you really need is water. In this regard, tap water is usually safe for drinking! Bottled water really is unnecessary! Also:

- Gas expense can be minimized by commuting once in a while. Walking or using your bike when doing small errands also helps.

- Do you really need that new cellular postpaid plan? Why not keep your old phone, minimize calls by texting, and consolidating your internet plan.

- Do you really need cable TV? Most of the things you watch anyway you can get online!

Things You Can't Skimp On

Regular home maintenance, auto insurance, tuition fees, taxes, regular medical checkups, etc. are things you cannot skimp on! Pay these on time and in full!

For example: Real estate insurance or other one time payments per annum must be factored into your expenses, divided into as many months, as the next installment. So if you still have 6 months to go, you can divide it in 6 monthly expense cycles. Never utilize your savings account for this. Your savings account is only to be used to pay debts and for emergencies.

Talk to Your Debtor

The last thing you want is to forget about the debt. The best thing to do is to talk to your creditor and ask for an extension. Even if this is not possible, keeping lines open can save you lots of troubles in the near future.

Freeze Interest Rates

If your creditor is a private person, maybe you can ask for an extension, without payment of interest. Explain your situation fully.

If your debtor is a bank or lending institution, there may be a grace period clause you can use. Although, be absolutely sure about using the grace period since this is most likely a onetime deal.

Switching debts

You can also ask if some demandable debts can be converted into a loan, i.e. A credit card debt converted to a personal bank loan. The interest rate is usually lower and you get to pay installments.

Mortgages

If you have a mortgage then you need to start thinking of how important that mortgage is to you and your capacity to pay. Your rule of thumb is to keep only what you can pay for and prioritize your needs.

For example

A family home is important, but if you cannot really afford the home then, maybe it's better to let go while you're able to. Do you really need that automobile? Remember you need to factor in amortizations, gas, upkeep, insurance, etc. If you can go to and from work via commute, then, maybe letting go of that car is the right thing to do.

If you have spare properties, then it is best to let go of the same to pay for debts. I.e. A second home, second automobile, expensive jewelry, etc.

But you need to learn when to let go and when to hang on to your properties. A good rule of thumb is to factor in interest payments and penalties. Then determine if lowering the asking price will allow you to save money or not.

To be perfectly honest, if you can pay your debts by selling peripheral or spare properties, then do it! But if selling your property only cuts less than 50% of your debts, then you need to look for other alternatives first.

Chapter 3: Viable Alternatives

Let us assume that you looked into your income and expense worksheet, you looked into your savings account, and you even factored in your real and personal properties. You've also contacted your relatives. But you are still short of paying "ALL" your debts. You need a little bit of help from a third party. Below are a few financial tools that you can utilize.

Real/Personal Property Mortgage

If you don't want to sell your property outright, you can mortgage it. Some authors will even tell you that taking out a second or third mortgage are alternatives. This author is of the opinion that you should NOT take out a second or third mortgage.

As a general rule, you stick to 1 mortgage per property. This is because; in most cases it will result in you making your debts more complicated! Best case scenario, you delay the demand ability of the debt. Worst case scenario, you lose another property, you get buried in more debt, more interest payments, and more penalties.

When mortgaging a property, always sign a deal on the winning side. This means you know you can handle the amortizations. You know you can keep the property. You know you can pay your debts in full.

Refinance

A refinance is a secondary mortgage that takes the place of the old mortgage. This can be from the same lender or different lender. A refinance is a viable alternative for those who are in a better position to renegotiate their loan terms. This includes, but is not limited to:

- A better credit report and score

- A better economy

- Promotional refinance rates

- A substantial down payment you've saved up

- You qualify for government mandated/regulated repayment plans

Fixed Rate All the Way

A caveat, you always want to know how much you will pay on the loan from the first amortization to the last amortization! So, whenever you apply for any loan or refinance your loan, it is almost always a good idea to make sure that your interest payments are fixed. Yes, there are a couple of exemptions wherein you can opt for adjustable rate mortgages and/or balloon payments, but these are very rare cases.

Debt Consolidation

Debt consolidation is a viable alternative for debtors who get confused by the many debts they have. Think about it, isn't it easier to pay just 1 loan with one interest rate and due once every month; as opposed to several loans, due on different dates, with different interest rates, from different lenders.

Aside from being convenient, lumping all your loans into one, may also afford you the advantage of a lower total interest rate. This means, the sum total of all your interest earning debts minus all your debtors, is higher, than the interest rate offered by a single lender.

It is always a good idea to consolidate "ALL" debts into one. But in some cases, you can leave out a couple of debts from the loan. It really is up to you and the advantages you can get form the consolidation.

No Longer Due

When you consolidate a loan, due debts become future debts. The total loan amount is divided into as many installments you and your lender agreed to. So you get a little bit of breathing room for at least a month.

More Onerous

Take note however, that one big debt is more destructive to your credit score, especially if it is a consolidation loan. This is not really a threat if you will be paying on time and in full. But if you default, then literally trouble begins to occur. Pay special attention to an acceleration clause. And at the very least, default in one consolidation loan and other lenders will be hesitant to provide you another one.

Simply put, this alternative is viable for a consumer who is in debt partly because of negligence, lack of skill in budgeting, and who might have experienced a temporary hardship in his/her finances.

Bankruptcy

There are several types of bankruptcy filing. This article will discuss the 2 most common types of private individuals, as debtors. Bear in mind that bankruptcy is not a magic pill. Not everyone is allowed to take it and not everyone will get "better" because of it. But if taken by the right consumer with proper planning and due execution, it can save you from overwhelming debt.

Means Test

This test initially determines what type of bankruptcy you can file for, or if you can file for one to begin with. The BK court will then assess the filer to determine if the BK will be allowed to prosper or should be dismissed.

Credit Rating and BK

There are a lot of "so called" experts who tell you that BK will ruin your credit report. News, flash, the fact that you are already buried in debt also ruins your BK. Yes your filing will make your credit score drop some more, but chances are, it will drop to that same low, even lower, if you keep bleeding due and demandable debts. Think of BK as an amputation of a limb. If you don't amputate, you'll die due to blood lost and or infection. The only plus side to a BK, is whatever you lose, you can eventually get back!

Yes, BK will last for 7 to 10 years depending on the type of BK and the length of the repayment plan. Within that same timeframe your facility of credit will be limited.

Lawyer of Self filing?

In theory, a person can file for BK without the help of a professional and/or lawyer. The forms and instructions are available for free via Bankruptcy courts, or online. In reality, only those with limited assets, "ALL" within the same state can realistically file for BK "pro se" (by themselves) i.e. a house, a car, some cash, etc. If you have several properties, some of which are out of state, then you need to at least hire professional and state licensed BK filers or lawyers.

Automatic Stay?

An automatic stay means creditors who do not hold a security over your property, cannot go after you, while your Bankruptcy filing is being heard by the BK court. Do not believe everything you hear. Yes, a BK filing can allow you to stop a bank from executing/foreclosing on your property, but only for the time being. This is because a bank or creditor has a mortgage or security clause that the BK court must respect. The best it can do is stay foreclosed for a couple of months. All the creditor does is file a petition in court showing a better right, then they can continue with the foreclosure.

Chapter 7

Also known as liquidation BK. As a general rule, any property not declared as exempt and not requested to be excluded is included in the BK filing. Chapter 7 is most applicable for those who have overwhelming debt, and have no capacity to pay.

Exceptions both as to type and amount depend on the state where you live. At the very least, a modest family home, unattached by any independent creditor can be exempted. So are modest clothing, furniture, professional articles, limited cash, etc.

Chapter 13

This is also known as repayment BK. The filer/debtor has financial capacity, but inability to pay the full amount of all debts. The creditors do not want to negotiate so the court steps in. Usually this involves cutting off the interest payments and penalties from all debts. Repayment usually lasts a couple to several years. While you are under repayment you need to pay on time and in full, lest your creditors find a hole they can exploit!

Chapter 4: Common Pitfalls (Get Rich Quick Schemes)

When trying to get out of debt, you need the right type of information, the right type of remedy, the proper plan of attack and a steady hand to follow thru until the last payment. The problem is, there are so many ways you can get things wrong. Below are a few things to steer clear of.

Who to Listen to

You don't want to listen to any Tom, Dick, or Harry. You want someone who has been there and done that! The author of this eBook is one such person. He started off as a debtor, crippled by credit card debts, a car loan, and a home mortgage. He was literally crawling form one paycheck to another. It took a while but eventually, all debts were paid.

Too Good to be True

It probably is! There is no easy way to get out of debt, especially substantial debt. You really need to tighten your belt and rack your brains. There is: no secret formula, no secret technique your creditors don't want you to know, no single tip that is so effective it should be illegal. Stay the course of paying your debts!

The Road You Take

Getting a refinance when in fact you know you are stretching things is a bad idea. Filing for BK when you can actually pay, will lead to a dismissal of your case. Tightening your budget when it is already so tight you are living a miserable life is also a bad idea. There are several financial tools you can utilize to get out of debt. Find that proper tool and utilize it!

Tip: consult with a credit counselor. The same counselor you will need a certificate from to file for BK. These individuals are state licensed and are neutral third parties. They can advice you on your viable alternatives based on your personal and financial situation.

Payday Loans

Simply put, payday lending is a bad idea. The interest rate is off the charts, and the ability to get instant cash is addictive to some individuals. And you have better alternatives. Chances are you still have a credit card, why not use that instead. But only in cases of emergencies!

Service Providers

You either buy a book to know what to do or hire the services of someone who will do everything for you. You don't buy a book with a service at a bloated cost, so someone can talk to you over the phone and "guide" you thru your problems. Heck, better call a credit counselor!

Chapter 5: Concentrate on Increasing Income

As mentioned earlier, you can only tighten the belt so much! You need to realize that you are budgeting to streamline your spending and to instill a discipline in yourself. When money is still short, and most probably it will be, then an additional source of income is the better alternative. Below are a few ideas.

Ask for a Salary Increase

If you come on time, rarely get absent, have excellent performance, then a raise is in order. Most companies have an assessment every 6 months to 2 years. When is your next assessment? Prepare for it! And make sure your company does provide for a salary increase.

Get a New Job

You'd be surprised that most debtors are employed. The problem is, they are under employed or are working on a dead end job. Here is a good rule of thumb. If you have been working for the same company for 3 years with no salary increase, with very little to do, and nothing important to contribute, then better get out! You want a job where you matter! Where you are part of the decision making! Where a salary increase for good performance is a sure thing!

Part Time Job

While you are looking for your dream job, you might as well augment your income by getting a part time job. The trend nowadays is to get an online job. This way you can go home, be with your kids, and still sneak in a couple of hours of work. If you are the man/woman of the house, then an online job allows you to add to your household's income, while still being able to take care of the kids or your elderly parents. Pick an online job that fits your skill and interest. You have dozens of options: transcription, teaching, back office documentation, auditing, content writing, website design and/or maintenance, marketing.

A Caveat

You are looking for an online job to make money, not part with your money! So steer clear of multi level marketing schemes, membership schemes, forex, bitcoin, stocks, etc. Simply put, anything that requires you to pay money first to get money is a no-no. No matter how tempting the offer is!

Chapter 6: Keep at It

Admit it, you are reading this eBook, thinking to yourself "This is easy, I can do that!" Yes you can! But several months into your well thought out plan, you start to cheat, with one credit card charge here, a new flagship android or Mac phone there, a designer pair of jeans here, and you're back to racking up debts!

Go back to your journal! Remember how bad things got! Don't let that happen again. You need to get to zero debt before making a substantial purchase! Heck, a smart phone can last you 3 to 5 years before it conks out. You're old jalopy can last even longer. Clothes, you can occasionally buy some, but only non signature brands and timed during big sale dates. You can splurge from time to time with food. This way you don't feel deprived, but only within reason and within budget!

Go Easy on the Credit Card

You do not need to cut your credit cards. At least, not unless you have more than three. Keep the most useful and oldest cards. Not necessarily the ones with the highest credit limit. Only use it for groceries, gas, and important purchases. Make use of the convenient points that you get.

Celebrate Milestones

Every month you successfully stick to your plan, order a box of pizza, or celebrate with a reasonably priced bottle of wine. Anything to tide you over for the long haul! This should keep your spirit up until you become debt free.

Chapter 7: Financial Education and Business Planning

Knowing how to handle your finances is a tricky endeavor. Sure you can do it by yourself, but it will be a trial and error thing. You have no time for that. While paying off your debts, look for worthwhile seminars. Nope, none of that universe crap! Get something more practical like accounting 101, consumer tax laws and how to use them to your advantage, or tax shielding, etc.

The Ultimate Goal

Remember, you want to be a millionaire, after you pay off your debts. How do you expect to handle that kind of money without proper schooling! At the very least, your financial education can provide you necessary certifications and contacts if and when you set up your own business!

Why Put Up a Business?

Your goal is to be a millionaire! The fastest way to that goal is thru your own business! So, what are you good at, what is your passion, what are you educated for? Remember that savings account? Aside from using that for your debt payments, you can also use that to put up a modest business.

Social Media Helps

Nowadays, a physical store location is no longer necessary. Put up shop at home. Make sure you have the appropriate certificates. Potential customers can visit you in a homey looking nook. Get some professional looking pictures. Don't pay someone; chances are you have a relative who has a professional grade camera! Now advertise online. Tap your family, relatives, friends, etc. Now use their social network to increase your coverage. Remember, your goal is to set up shop with minimal capital outlay. Most of your funds should be used for your goods, or inventory!

Tip: put up a dedicated page for your business. Link social media outlets like Facebook, twitter, Instagram, SalesForce, LinkedIn etc.

Simple Value

All you need is a product that meets a certain human need. It has to be cheaper, do things better, or in a different way than your competition. Now run with it! Try a viral ad campaign on YouTube, Instagram, tweeter, etc. now set up several ads, and see what works and what does not.

Price Wars?

If you don't have a unique product, or if there are other sellers who have a different version of your product, the last thing you want is to cut prices to try and undermine the competition. This can lead to a price war that is bad for business. What you should do is try to carve your own following. Remember, with the social media generation it's all about lifestyle and branding.

Go Local First

Identify your product or service with your locality. Again use social media to carve out a local following. This should set you apart from out of town and state sellers/services. Personally interact with buyers. This increases your support and the information you get can be useful in version 2 of your product and/or service.

Go to Conventions

Visit conventions showcasing your business. Get ideas from them! See if you can widen your product or service base with some of the ideas and contacts you get from that convention. Your next step is to put up shop in a convention hall.

Conclusion

Thank you again for purchasing this book!

I hope this book was able to help you to: realize that there is a way out of overwhelming debt; you need to outfit yourself with the right tools, and execute the right plan; you need to follow thru until you have zero debt; and, you need to step things up a notch and augment your income!

The next step is to go back to your journal. Re-read the eBook to get more insight, add some more notes. Now consult with a debt counselor! Pay the minimal fee, and make sure to get the certificate you need, just in case you need to file for BK in the near future.

Remember, getting out of debt is not a race. It is a marathon that requires mental toughness and endurance. You should pace yourself, don't run out of steam midway thru!

Finally, if you enjoyed this book, please take the time to share your thoughts and post a review on Amazon. We do our best to reach out to readers and provide the best value we can. Your positive review will help us achieve that. It'd be greatly appreciated!

Thank you and good luck!

Book 2:

Money Marketing Mastery

BY J.J.JONES

Successful Strategies to Mastering Marketing to Make Money!

Copyright 2014 J.J.Jones - All rights reserved.

In no way is it legal to reproduce, duplicate, or transmit any part of this document in either electronic means or in printed format. Recording of this publication is strictly prohibited and any storage of this document is not allowed unless with written permission from the publisher. All rights reserved.

Table Of Contents

Introduction

I want to thank you and congratulate you for purchasing the book, *"Money Marketing Mastery: Successful Strategies to Mastering Marketing to Make Money!"*

This book contains proven steps and strategies on how to start your marketing career and how to get started to earn more money right now.

Marketing is a lucrative career that you can take if you want a recession-proof and steady of source of income right in the comforts of your home. The internet has provided practically limitless opportunities for marketers to take their careers to the next level without having to spend years of service in marketing companies and other businesses that require traditional marketing services. Today, one of the leading online businesses is internet marketing.

As internet marketing promises the biggest opportunity of making money to today's modern businessmen, this book focuses on the different strategies of mastering marketing to make money starting from scratch up to proper marketing management to gain bigger market share; hence, more money.

As a modern marketer, you will practically promote, sell and refer products and services by other businesses, although you can also market your own products and service but with a different income structure. Once you commit to do marketing, you have to dedicate your time and resources as you will be doing practically everything, from the selection of products and services, doing the marketing research and applying market studies, creating media and marketing materials, identifying markets, interacting with customers and potential markets, to closing a deal and collecting and collating customer feedbacks as part of your market research. A modern marketer is his own team.

In general, you can also apply the tips that will be given here to your own e-commerce business if you manage your own online store or run an actual office-based business with internet marketing arm.

This early, you need to understand that marketing is not as simple as writing an ad or review and posting it in your own blog. Marketing is more complex than that. It is holistic. It needs time and patience because unlike direct selling, it tries to reach larger markets by maximizing various media. If you are up for the challenge, then proceed with the next chapter.

Thanks again for purchasing this book, I hope you enjoy it!

Chapter 1 - Choosing a Promising Product

"Promising" either means the product having a huge market demand with high potential for expansion to other market segments, or a product with high potential to create a demand (like in the case of innovative and unique products). Choosing a product to market is the first strategy towards building a successful career in marketing, whether you choose to venture in affiliate marketing, network marketing, multilevel marketing (MLM), online marketing, attraction marketing, email marketing, direct marketing or social media marketing.

Unfortunately, many marketing novices fail to throw sufficient attention in the products themselves. Rather, they look at their projected earnings, which is not really surprising because earning is their main goal in the first place.

Choosing a good, sellable product is the first important step of starting your marketing career because all your effort will be futile if you will keep on pushing with a product that has no market to begin with. The product and business you are marketing for should meet high standards that make them credible, reputable and reliable. Otherwise, you are just bating yourself for scammers to take advantage.

Investing your time and money on high-paying yet substandard and questionable affiliate programs, networking businesses and MLM structures will cost you more than what you invest; it will cost you your own name, reputation and everything that you work hard for just to get a place in the cutthroat world of the marketing industry where everyone seems to rebuke and malign tough competitors to steal their shares.

Remember that no marketing strategy can save you if the product itself fails to meet the expectations of consumers. On the other hand, a high quality product only needs minimal marketing efforts as its standard sell for itself.

In choosing a product to sell or marketing program to join, consider these six essential factors that determine the probability of your success in the marketing business.

- **Demand.** Also called the gravity of product, there should be an existing market demand, or at least, promising direction, for a type of product before anybody can claim potential for success. This means choosing a relatively new product with not much track record of success as your affiliate product comes with high risk.

  If you think that it is promising but still has no solid market-base just yet, it might be a wiser decision to venture on article marketing, attraction marketing, blogging, direct marketing, SEO marketing or social media marketing instead of affiliate marketing because these types of marketing are more equipped for introductory campaigns than affiliate marketing.

- **High commission.** The point of being a marketer is earning. It is but natural to look for opportunities that pay well. For instance, affiliate marketers normally earn from 4% to 25% of the total selling price of whatever products they are marketing. The commission rates can change depending on demand, average price range, market distribution and product type.

  Affiliate products and services with higher demands normally have lower commission rates because they are easier to market anyway. On the other hand, those that are normally selling at high prices, such as lawn mowers and industrial humidifiers, come with higher commissions because they are harder to market. If a product can be bought from a lot of sources (such as when there are already a lot of affiliate marketers for a particular affiliate program), the commission is also higher because the competition is stiffer.

  Nonetheless, if a company thinks that its affiliate product has high potential for success yet still does not have decent demand, it might give high commission simply to attract more marketers for them.

- **Impressive bonuses and more opportunities.** Affiliate programs usually provide bonuses for excellent performances and sales thresholds, while some offer opportunities to market for bigger commission rates and head a team of their own. These are extra motivators for their affiliates to work harder. Bonuses might include monetary rewards, free products, electronic vouchers, gift certificates, all-expense paid local and foreign trips, free trainings and seminars or leadership positions where they can earn more and be paid with honoraria for managing a team.

  Excellent performances might mean consistent level of referrals, outstanding marketing strategies, innovative marketing and selling techniques or excellent customer feedbacks. For sales threshold, companies usually set non-requirement quotas and commission levels. Hence, dedication and investment of time are necessary if you want to build a solid career in the affiliate marketing industry.

- **Decent return rate**. Return rate means the projected return on investment (ROI) for all the expenditures you might incur, such as websites, paid advertisements, outsourcing requirements, resellers, etc. It can also mean the return of your investment computed for every product you are marketing (your expense per product on periodical basis).

  The actual return rate will be determined by your ability to market and dedication to the work, but companies also have computed return rates that they promise to their affiliates by taking into consideration the maximal or minimal possible sales volumes a marketer can handle per day. This is why you see networking and MLM companies advertise how much their members can earn on a daily or weekly basis.

If a company promises high return rate, the data they used probably comes from the average return rates of their existing affiliates. There are companies that guarantee specific return rates within given period but they are usually the ones that collect membership fees upon applications.

- **High payout and proper payout ceiling.** There should be an existing data where average payouts could be based from. How much can you earn within a particular period? How much can you earn by volume and by hitting thresholds? How much commissions have the company already paid during their entire operation? You need to have an idea of your projected earning for every cumulative effort you will give.

  Likewise, the payout ceiling should not be too low so as not to be an inconvenience should you be very successful with your marketing business. At the same time, it should not be too hard to hit, so you can withdraw easier and faster.

  You also have to consider the terms of payment and methods used. A popular method is wiring through Paypal or directly to a bank account, but some still employ traditional payouts, like in the case of Google for its Adsense (not an affiliate program) where check is still the only option.

- **Reputation of the product and company.** It only needs common sense. Why would you join a marketing program with suspicious promises and rewards, or market products with questionable qualities and benefits? However, as simple as it might seem, there are still people who venture in affiliate programs and networking businesses without actually looking into reputation and credibility. They fall as victims to scams and illegitimate businesses in the end.

  Promised rewards and commission rates are too tempting sometimes that people would no longer consider other factors but the earning potentials. However, projected incomes are mere figures in writing, and they do not necessarily translate to actual payouts if the company does not have the ability and resources to deliver their promises in the first place.

  You need to look at the company's credibility amongst other marketers, such as affiliates, bloggers, networkers, etc. A simple online research will lead you to a lot of reviews and accounts of actual experiences. Ask around to safeguard your interest.

  Also look at the company's operation if they have already been tested by time and unfortunate circumstances. You do not want to earn thousands of dollars in commission just to lose it before payout simply because the company has already gone out of business.

  It also pays to check the reputation of the product, in particular, because there is a possibility that it already has impending negative image in the media or market. This is most especially true for food supplements and fitness equipment.

Some affiliate marketers do everything to promote certain types of food supplements for months just to discover that the latest scientific research about their products refute their effectiveness and safety. It happened to a lot of weight loss supplements before, where their potencies turned out to be nothing but mere marketing hypes.

- **Niche.** What is your line of specialization – your strengths and expertise? What are your interests that you think you can make you fulltime career? Narrow down your best picks and stick to a particular nature of interest; that will be your niche. Sticking with your niche is important because you have to establish authority and reputation in a specific field to become credible and reliable.

Creating a niche market is more important for marketers who sell ideas, contents and information, like in the case of bloggers, SEO marketers and article marketers. No one believes a know-it-all claim, so it will just be your own downfall to market everything there is under the sun without a clear path to take. By involving yourself in a line you are not familiar with, you are also taking the risk of losing interest in the end, rendering everything you built useless.

Do not jump to health and nutrition even if your line is automotives simply because an affiliate referred you to an affiliate program with high commission rate.

Choose your niche based on your actual knowledge and interest and not merely based on the opportunities awaiting you. As an affiliate, networking, multilevel, email, direct or social media marketer, you have to choose the product you are going to promote coming from your niche. Do not let every butterfly flying your direction get your attention. There will be a lot of opportunities in the marketing industry, but the real question will always be which one you can justify and commit to.

Chapter 2 – Finding What to Market

Now you know how to choose a product to market, but do you know how and where to find it? Finding is the hardest part because there are a lot of ideas everywhere and a lot of products to choose from. Of course, you can always do it the hard way of randomly researching different affiliate and networking sites on all possible sources, but that will eat up a lot of your time spent unwisely.

The best way to find the right product for you is by going directly to the sources. Consider this as the first part of your market research. Here are the best sources you can try.

Blogs and forums

Blogs and forums are reliable sources because people are talking about their actual experiences there, encouraging more discussions for other readers to see the pros and cons of each marketing program and product. These sites are open to refuting and confirmations, so their information are more credible than affiliate and networking sites that use marketing materials for contents. They are the perfect venues to cross-check for accuracy because they are updated, interactive and straightforward.

Go to blogs and forums sites then type "affiliate marketing," "network marketing," "MLM," "multilevel marketing," "home business," "online opportunity," or "income opportunity" in their search boxes, but you can also be specific by searching for the marketing program, product or company you are interested to join. It is certain that you have a lot of readings to do, but just be patient for your own sake.

Keyword research tools and analytics

These online tools are reliable aid for market research because they feed accurate and real-time information based on the actual movements of the market – the more than two billion people who go online everyday worldwide, who also spend more than $2.1 billion on affiliate marketing products alone. They analyze and crunch data according to actual search inputs of netizens in search engines. That means you identify specific trends and interests of your possible market segments that can also be narrowed down by locations. You will know what they want and what they are willing to spend for in advance.

News websites and peer-review journals

Look at trends and possible trends based on the latest scientific research and news, then, hype them up a bit by making these sources look like endorsements. Throw in some celebrity statements that you will interpret as endorsements, and you are up for a marketing homerun.

The medical and scientific communities are the most reliable sources of possible trends in the health and wellness industry. This encompasses the nutrition, fitness, food and beverage industries. Unfortunately, most of the time, scientific researches are preempted by manufacturing and processing companies that hype up inconclusive yet promising results. This is practically how manufacturers of dietary supplements get their clues and cues to penetrate larger markets and create more hype.

Researchers naturally look for potential treatments for various diseases, so they put to test dozens of natural chemical compounds, herbal plants and fruits, minerals and anything that might take medical science one step higher. Normally, a research takes years or even decades to complete, but businesses always find ways to create hype and earn money from it.

When scientists say that a fruit has a compound that can strengthen the immune system to fight cancer, businessmen can go around that and say the fruit can fight cancer. Technically speaking, it is not an illegal act since dietary supplements are labeled as "No Therapeutic Claim." Right there, a new lucrative product is born.

By looking at research journals, you can determine existing food supplements and other nutritional products that have high potential for business. Using article marketing, SEO marketing, attraction marketing, blogging and social media marketing, you can create demand when there is none.

News websites and magazines are also excellent media where you can find promising products because they are well-researched with insider information. You can bank on their resources by using their reports as your basis and support. Similarly, medical bulletins and shows also make for good sources. Ask Dr. Oz why he's always used as a source for marketing materials.

Direct Selling Association

Direct selling is not be mistaken for direct marketing, the former employing direct sellers dealing with and reaching customers vis-a-vis. However, if there is one group who knows a lot about direct marketing, affiliate marketing, network marketing and multilevel marketing, it would be the Direct Selling Association of America or the World Federation of Direct Selling Associations (WFDSA).

These organizations keep track of their member companies, so they know which ones make money and which ones have bigger potentials. Although these companies are classified as direct selling companies, they also use affiliate marketing, network marketing and MLM to expand their markets. As a matter of fact, networking is practically the principle behind their operations.

By looking at their top performers and member companies with unique and innovative products, you will get a bigger picture of the market trends and marketing trends. Most of them also accept affiliates and networkers, so you might just land on a good deal for your marketing career.

Online marketplace

These are sites that hold digital information products that are marketed by affiliates and those wanting to start a career in affiliate marketing. In the simplest sense, businesses that have products to sell hire marketers by placing their products under these online marketplaces, which does the hiring, promotion and compensation to all of its members.

The largest online marketplace today that you should check is Clickbank that holds a collection of more than 46,000 products for affiliate marketers to promote. It has attracted more than 1.5 million affiliates and has claimed to pay $2,000,000,000 in commissions in a single year alone. Clickbank has marketing presence in more than 200 countries, so your marketing career can expand across continents.

Other trustworthy online marketplaces to check out are Commission Junction, PayDotCom (spelled as is) and Linkshare.

Manufacturer's website

This is a basic way to become a marketer for businesses – by looking for products you want and think you can market, and going directly to their official websites to inquire for an affiliate or networking opportunity.

Many companies welcome registrations of marketers through their websites. Just look for the "Affiliate" section or button, then, register online. There might also be other variety of income opportunity that you can find.

For businesses that are not open to third party marketers just yet, you might want to inquire on the possibility of being their reseller instead. You won't get a certain percentage as commission, but you can resell products on prices of your own accord. This way, you will be marketing for the profit.

Online store

Amazon, Barnes and Noble and other online stores have their own bestselling lists – direct hints of what is marketable and what is not. These lists are more useful if you are registered as an affiliate of these sites.

For instance, Amazon has its own affiliate program in which interested individuals can register and be an affiliate with no commitment at all. Its affiliates simply need to promote products coming from its hundreds of thousands of available affiliate products with commissions starting from 4% to 20%, and close a successful sale. Amazon affiliates can ensure higher sales rate by promoting bestselling products that are already marketable and sellable by themselves. They offer bestselling lists for hundreds of categories, from kitchen faucets to computer tablets.

Even Yahoo! keeps track of bestselling items in certain categories. Whenever you have doubts about the marketability of your products, just verify them with bestselling lists. You can never go wrong with actual sales rank.

Review sites

Many review websites now hire their own affiliates because they also earn through referral fees. Naturally, products with better reviews have stronger market appeal. By sticking with well-received products, you are guaranteed with quality offerings that you will be proud to promote.

Many review sites also have rundown lists based on review scores. These are as reliable as bestselling lists or even better because you have more room to push further with your marketing tactics.

Chapter 3 – Jumpstarting Your Marketing Career

The next step to establishing a successful career in the marketing industry is starting the actual venture itself. This is the stage where you put all your plans and ideas into use by executing them through preparation and actual operation.

The biggest question at this point is how you will promote the products or services you have to market. Here are marketing strategies you can follow.

1. Set up a well-navigable website designed for SEO marketing

As a marketer, your website is your office, helpdesk, hotline, showroom, catalogue sales office, advertisement, billboard and practically everything you need to successfully fulfill your marketing tasks. Thus, it needs to be organized, clean, responsive, substantial and attractive.

A website has to be designed for function and not attraction because an attractive website is not necessarily functional and user-friendly while the latter is apt to be attractive. The internal navigation should be clear and easily accessible from the home page, feeding your readers with peeks of what your website is all about. The layout and design should also be controlled and reasonable.

The danger of designing your own website without sufficient knowledge is making it look like amateur, like a novice blogger trying to draw attention using uncoordinated colors, screaming animations and effects, impractical font styles and colors, inconsistent styles and themes and worse, misleading internal linking. Many bloggers usually use any designing feature they can add when creating a website. However, that does not really make their websites attractive but questionable.

Extravagant websites like an online carnival is seen by netizens as red flag because that is a practice commonly done by online scams. Have you ever noticed why "money-making" websites use screaming font sizes just to say you can be rich or make money within this and that period? Or display exaggerated testimonials complete with profiles and exact figures right at the home pages? These are websites designed for attraction and not function, and they are likely a scam, a scam you do not want to be identified with.

2. Choose the best domain name for your marketing venture

As a marketer, your domain is your business card and direct line. All your marketing efforts are practically centered in maximizing the capacity of your domain to attract new markets and reach out to your existing ones. Your email marketing, direct marketing, SEO marketing, blogging and social media marketing efforts practically end and goes back to your domain name – the location of your office that is your website. You might be surprised but many marketers only concentrate their efforts and attention on building the reputation of their domain names because at the end of the day, people will remember not your name but your domain name.

Some businesses buy already acquired domain names for as long as the addresses are guaranteed to bring in millions of visitors – and potential customers – back to their business sites and sales page. Similarly, many private individuals already buy domain names of businesses and trends that are likely to pick up and gain massive success in the future.

Attraction plays a very important role in rounding up your own market. Like on almost all businesses, their names are their most important attractions, and your own business name or brand should be clearly reflected in your domain name, or simply your website address. This is your face amongst millions of internet habitués – something that you will be remembered for even before they try out your product or service.

Although domain name does not compose everything that is to be considered for your search engine result page ranking, it will still count in your race to the top of search engines as algorithms first examine domain names in assessing the relevance of a site to a particular keyword/s that is being searched. It will also be your starting point in building your social media presence as your home pages and website should all be well-coordinated, both in name and content.

In choosing the best domain name for your marketing venture, you have to choose a name that best represents your product, service or content without sacrificing branding. Your domain name should clearly represent what you have to offer, dropping the hint at first glance, as much as possible. However, you have to be specific without sacrificing your brand.

A catering service located in Glendale can be easily found online with a domain name called *www.glendalecateringservices.com*. However, a very generic domain will ironically make you suffer obscurity, making you just another home business trying to make money but not offer a difference.

Usually, the product and service are already made obvious in the business name, which can also be the registered name or the trademark, like *Heaven Scent* for perfume business and *Bellisima Baby Bags* for, what else, but baby bags. The business name then becomes the domain name.

Mixing your own brand with a generic representation makes you standout and more memorable. It also makes it easier for you to find an available domain name that you can buy.

3. Generate marketing leads

Leads are the possible destinations of your messages, the receivers of your marketing efforts, and possibly, your customers. Once you already have the leads, starting your plans will be a lot easier. The hardest part, though, is getting your hands on that list.

You can collect your own marketing leads by keeping track of your analytics and checking out if some of them visit you under their social media accounts and blogs. You can approach them easier if you know what they are looking for in particular.

You can also leave a registration box in your site where interested visitors can leave their contact details, mostly emails, for your updates. Send them newsletters and activate feeds, so you can keep track of them and stay in touch. By creating threads in your comment sections, you can also identify specific people who are potentially your own followers.

There are existing market-databases that brokers sell to marketers. These brokers are marketers themselves who already collected marketing leads of their own through networks and years of marketing efforts. They sell these leads, but not all of them sell usable marketing leads for your own niche, of course. The Direct Selling Association of America has its own brokers who sell lists of possible customers together with their contact details to member companies and sales agents. You might want to have connection with an insider to have access to that.

Lastly, there are also software and online tools that generate marketing leads by collecting static information in the internet, producing you names, email addresses and phone numbers, while some sold tools already have existing market-databases. Usually, these software and tools scan other existing websites and blogs for contact details, then, feed the collected data to you. It is up to you how to use those contact details.

4. Maximize online forums

Forums are also a great tool in doing your market research because of the volume of customer feedbacks you can get from them. You go at the center of their discussions to determine the key issues customers want to be addressed. Some of your most reliable marketing leads can also come from these threads because you can already analyze the reception of your market through interaction.

By stirring interest through discussions, you can also establish yourself as an expert that is credible, reliable and knowledgeable of what people are looking for and interest in. Offer your service by giving advice and helping others. This is a fast way to redirect curious parties straight to your website. By establishing yourself amongst a circle of people with similar interests, you also make it easier to penetrate their consciousness and sell without them knowing.

It is easier to influence your market when you already gained their trust and loyalty, and that is only possible by letting them think that you are beneficial to them in any way possible.

Conclusion

Thank you again for purchasing this book!

I hope this book was able to help you to start your marketing career the best way possible.

The next step is to start following the tips given here and practicing them with utmost commitment.

Finally, if you enjoyed this book, please take the time to share your thoughts and post a review on Amazon. We do our best to reach out to readers and provide the best value we can. Your positive review will help us achieve that. It'd be greatly appreciated!

Thank you and good luck!

Check Out My Other Books

Below you'll find some of my other popular books that are popular on Amazon and Kindle as well. Simply click on the links below to check them out. Alternatively, you can visit my author page on Amazon to see other work done by me.

Marketing Money Mastery

http://amzn.to/1hxUaj6

"Debt Free Forever"

http://amzn.to/1qrgldh

Money Management Makeover

http://amzn.to/1hAU8Z7

Single Women and Budgets

http://amzn.to/WPRJ3M

www.ingramcontent.com/pod-product-compliance
Lightning Source LLC
Chambersburg PA
CBHW070725180526
45167CB00004B/1627

* 9 7 8 1 5 0 3 3 6 9 0 5 4 *